Jordan Vicky Harrison worked in the film industry for many years as a script supervisor. After the birth of her daughter Lauren, she became a teacher working with autistic children. Although she has a BA in Art History, she is a science geek who loves to explore space and time. She is an avid traveller, foodie, dog lover and likes nothing better than spending time in the great outdoors with her daughter.

This book is dedicated to my daughter, Lauren, who is a constant source of all things nice.

OUTRAGEOUS RHYMES

BY

Jordan Harrison

AUSTIN MACAULEY PUBLISHERS®

LONDON • CAMBRIDGE • NEW YORK • SHARJAH

A CIP catalogue record for this title is available from the British Library.

ISBN 9781398470743 (Paperback)
ISBN 9781398470750 (ePub e-book)

www.austinmacauley.com

First Published 2024
Austin Macauley Publishers Ltd®
1 Canada Square
Canary Wharf
London
E14 5AA

I would like to thank Lauren who had to listen to me drone on through various stages of rhyme. At times, the rhyming couplets leeched into everyday speech. I would like to thank Carlo Collodi for inventing *Pinocchio*; Charles Perrault for *Cinderella* and *Sleeping Beauty*; Robert Southey for *Goldilocks and the Three Bears* and Giambattista Basile and the Grimm Brothers for *Rumpelstiltskin* whose fairy tales are not only brilliant but also worthy of tomfoolery. I never had the opportunity to meet the great Stephen Hawkins but I hope he would appreciate my *Big Bang* poem, and Kew Gardens for the fabulous *Palm House* where one of the poems is set.

Table of Contents

Celia, the Pig

Pigs are pink and smelly too,
But Celia was a shade of blue.
She hated mud. She hated mess,
She found her life a real test.

Unlike her friends,
She had no time,
For rolling round in mud and slime.
Instead she liked to swim a lot,
In fact she didn't give a jot.

When farmer Parsnip came to look,
He found her writing in a book.
"Good God," he said,
"That pig's my ticket.
Let's call the press,
There's money in it!
We'll charge a pound for all to see,
This wonderful anomaly."

They came in coaches, bikes and motors,
They came with cameras and took their photos.
The money it came flooding in,

But Celia found it rather grim.
She hated all the noise and fuss,
Her plan was swift: *"I'll catch the bus."*

She dodged the crowds and jumped the gate,
"It's time to leave. Don't stop me, mate!"
The double-decker looked just fine,
"Let's hope the driver likes his swine?"

She sat upstairs to admire the view,
"I need a change, completely new."
Then all at once the idea hit,
"I know – I'll make a career of it.

Interior design will make me rich,
They'll like me blue; it's very kitsch.
I'll call my shop 'Miss Piggy Sue',
That's bound to make the blue rinse coo.
I'll design the sofas, curtains the lot,
I'll create the garden; it'll be so hot."

So Celia did as she had planned,
The moral being that pigs aren't bland!

Georgette, the Pet

Elephants can be pets, you know,
In fact they've been in many a show.
You can train them like a dog or cat,
They can sit and beg if you want that.
The only problem which can arise,
Is due in part to their enormous size!
You see – you cannot be complacent,
With a friend the size of someone's basement.
One slip and you'll be squashed to pulp,
A fact that made poor Georgette gulp!
It happened one fine and sunny day,
When little Roland came to play.
Georgette came bounding over on call,
When she slipped and skidded to the wall.
Little Roland never stood a chance,
He spun around as if in a dance.
But unable to move with any haste,
Was crushed and pulped into a paste.
Poor Georgette hung her head in shame,
And even though she wasn't to blame,
She made a vow right there and then,
That if she found a friend again.
She'd take more time to move around,
And slowly walk along the ground.
The memory of Roland faded away,

And at last a new friend came to play.
"Hello," said Connie, all pretty and bright,
"I need a friend if that's alright?"
Those words were nectar to Georgette's ears,
And keeping her vow, she slowly appeared.
Unfortunately, what she didn't see,
Was a tiny mouse near Connie's knee.
As Georgette approached her newfound friend,
The mouse began to jump and wend.
It let out a squeak for all to hear,
And Georgette stopped in absolute fear.
She reared up to the size of a house,
Then dropped back down to squash the mouse.
Poor Connie she had stood too near,
And had no time to disappear.
The mouse and Connie were squashed to bits,
Georgette was good at direct hits.
"That elephants a killer!" shouted a man,
"That's two kids down – let's escape while we can."
Georgette came over to explain,
But got her foot caught in the drain.
And then with an almighty thump,
She tripped and fell upon a lump.
On closer inspection, it became quite clear,
The lump was the man escaping in fear.
The keeper looked into the cage,
Then flew into a nasty rage.
"You killer beast, what have you done?"
Georgette knew it was time to run.
She charged with all her strength and might,
And disappeared into the night.

Then fate turned up to play its hand,
As Georgette crossed some open land.
A little girl came running along,
And tripped and fell into the pond.
Georgette charged over to save the day,
Plopped in her trunk and sucked away.
The water level fell quite fast,
And the little girl was found at last.
"That elephant's a hero," the mother cried,
"She'll be safe with you by her side."
So Georgette and Lucy lived happily ever after,
And their lives were full of fun and laughter.

Homework

"A school can be extremely silly,"
Came the resounding cry from my Uncle Willy.
"They never seem to understand,
That doing homework is always bland!
For goodness sake – it stands to reason,
That extra work must count as treason.
Evening time is for fun and glee,
Not extra lessons in geography.
Surely being at school from eight to four,
Is longer than many work, I'm sure.
But to add another couple more,
Seems to break THE CHILD PROTECTION LAW!"

Mrs Smith

Mrs Smith,
Mrs Smith,
How lovely you look

Mrs Smith,
Mrs Smith,
I'll read your book

Mrs Smith,
Mrs Smith,
Why is Benjamin crying?

Mrs Smith,
Mrs Smith,
Please stop him – keep trying

Mrs Smith,
Mrs Smith,
You're not stopping him bawl

Mrs Smith,
Mrs Smith,
You're not lovely at all!

Goldilocks and the Three Bears

This little girl with golden hair,
Had entered the wood without a care.
She was rather dim – not very bright,
In several hours, it would be night.
As predicted by my sombre tone,
Goldilocks roamed too far from home.
Her tummy rumbled – she felt quite sick,
The trees were getting very thick!
Then just within the nick of time,
She came upon a smell divine.
So using her most developed sense,
She followed the smell to a nearby fence.
Beyond she saw a house so fine,
That's my ticket, she thought. *In there I'll dine.*
So quickly she approached to look inside,
Stood by the window and started to whine.
Then realising there was no reply,
She straightened up and lost the cry.
She pushed the door – it opened fast,
"Sanctuary," she said, *"at last."*
Three bowls of porridge stood nearby,
But which one should she start to try?
"I'll go for the biggest," she said in greed,
But the heat of the porridge made her gums bleed.
"Let's try the middle one – I'll be very bold,

Oh my God! It's really cold."
Feeling very despondent and rather small,
She picked up the final bowl of all.
It tasted delicious – she couldn't get enough,
With her tummy full, she felt less rough.
She crossed the room and sat on the largest chair,
It was hard to reach and she dangled there.
"It's far too hard!" she shouted without a care,
"I know; let's try the middle chair."
Immediately, she sank into the cushions stacked high,
"I can't sit here – I'll suffocate and die!"
So she turned to the smallest chair of all,
Which she broke as she sat and began to fall.
"Ouch!" she screamed as she hit the floor,
Then she marched out the room and slammed the door!

"I think it's time to go to bed,
I really need to rest my head."
Her past experience had taught her nil,
So the largest bed she scaled like a hill.
Oh damn! she thought, *it's far too hard,*
I'd rather sleep in my backyard.
Let's try the middle one – just to see,
But I bet it'll be far too soft for me!"
Indeed it was, and she set off to find,
If the smaller bed would be more kind?

Very soon she fell into a lovely sleep,
But was unaware of a voice that was very deep.
"Who's been eating my porridge?" asked the Daddy bear,
But got no reply, as his wife didn't care!
She was far more concerned with what came into sight,
Her bowl of porridge had been tampered with, alright!
Then the baby bear gave out a gurgling plea,
"My bowl is empty – will someone FEED ME?"
On closer inspection, the chairs came into sight,
And sympathy lies with the baby bear's plight.
He loving grabbed at his pieces of chair,
Then sent up a growl which filled the air.
In the bedroom above Goldilocks began to alight,
As she started to realise that things were not right.
Up the stairs came the family all exceedingly cross,
And Daddy bear growled just to show he was boss.
From room to room the inspection passed,
Then they came to the little bear's room at last.
The baby bear screamed, *"There's a girl in my bed!"*
"Quick, get her," said Dad. *"She'll be tastier dead!"*
Goldilocks leapt out of the window and ran out of sight,
Escaping the bears as she felt they might bite.
And the MORAL here is easy to see,
It's more of an issue of HEALTH and SAFETY.
Always remember to lock the door after you,
Or you could end up with a Goldilocks too.

Shark for Tea

The shark thinks he is good at fishing,
But I feel part of his brain's missing.

He was easy to bait with bits of fish,
Then cooked and served as a local dish!

Belly, Belly, Mr Kelly

Silly, silly, Mr Kelly,
Had the most enormous belly.
He ate ten meals each and every day,
That's how his belly got that way.

Bacon for breakfast,
And brunch and tea,
Then ham and pork crackling,
Whenever he was free.

Treats galore at every single break,
Especially his favourite chocolate cake.
He'd have it piled upon his plate,
Then he ate and ate and ate and ate.

The doctor came to call one day,
And told Mr Kelly the price he'd pay.
Your heart will find it hard to cope,
With all that fat, you silly dope!

But as always, Mr Kelly ignored,
Without his food, he would get bored.
So more and more he piled on his plate,
And happy Mr Kelly ate and ate.

But what he hadn't wanted in life,
Was to settle down and take a wife.
Alas! That was all about to change,
As Mr Kelly became deranged.

After one particularly enormous meal,
Mr Kelly decided he didn't feel.
The way he normally felt at night,
Clearly, something here just wasn't right!

He called an ambulance for help,
And the nurse in charge let out a YELP.
"What made you become this enormous size?
Such gluttony cannot be wise."

So nurse Ethel, in her wily way,
Put Kelly on a diet that day.
Then bit by bit they fell in love,
They seemed to fit just like a glove.

Now Mr Kelly was in a mood,
Was it Ethel for him or was it food?
The choice was really hard to make,
As his mind went back to his chocolate cake.

He had lost some weight – in fact five stones,
He thought he looked like skin and bones.
He missed his belly and beloved food,
So Mr Kelly began to brood.

This made him very sick indeed,
So Ethel was forced to intercede.
You can have your food, you silly man,
Just don't give up – I know you can!

Then looking in her sobbing eyes,
Helped him at last to realise,
That this woman was the thing for him,
He didn't care if he was thin!

Too Late

I had hoped to visit my great Aunt Flossy,
Even though she was extremely bossy.
But – much to my complete dismay,
I found she died the other day!

Don't Wash Your Hair in Glue

You must never wash your hair in glue,
It's not a sensible thing to do.
But should you act so very thick,
Just remember that the towel will stick.

Pea Soup

Pea soup is nutritious, my mother said,
"Eat it – or you'll go to bed."
Since tiredness had already taken its toll,
I said, "Goodnight," and passed my bowl.

Peace

It's hard to know – why so much din,
I crave a place with peace within.
My brother and sister make a noise,
While always playing with their toys.
At school, there's always so much to do,
For peace, I sit upon the loo.
But even there you hear girls chat,
Nothing important – just this and that.
Surely, others must agree,
I can't believe it's only me.
Who longs to escape this eternal din?
And find that inner peace within.

Grandparents

My mother's mum and dad are old,
And their hands are always freezing cold.

Each time when Grandma comes to tea,
The first request is: *"I need to wee."*
Apparently, this happens with age,
Which sends my grandpa into a rage?
"You've just arrived – how can you go already?"
Then he stomps his feet – he's not that steady.
"Stop complaining," Grandma starts to spit,
"You're such a whinny silly old git!"
Then they spend the day calling each other names,
So I ask if we could play some games.
"That would be lovely," Grandma replies,
I can tell her voice is full of lies.
The last thing she must want to do,
Is sit for hours without the loo?

But, true to her word, she plays with me,
First snakes and ladders, then monopoly.
And with each and every move she makes,
My grandpa points out her mistakes.
"NO, don't buy Mayfair – it's much too dear,
They'll be lots of tax to pay, I fear."
"Just go away, and let me be,
This game is just for Tom and me."
To no avail – they never part,
Such constant snipping is an art.
When eventually it's time to eat,
I rush to the table and take my seat.
I chose the chair near my mum and dad,
Which makes my grandma very sad?
"Oh, don't sit there, you silly lad,
Move near to me – swap with your dad!"
So once again, I'm with the old folk,
My patience is failing – it's not a joke.
Then as Mother tries to pass the peas,
My grandpa starts to joke and tease.
"Don't eat too many of those, my dear,
Or you'll be running to the loo, I fear."
This is the final straw for my Grandma Joan,
Who responded with an enormous groan.
Then grabbing the dish of passing peas,
She threw them on my grandpa's knees.
"Good God, what did you do that for?"
But Grandma Joan had reached the door.
"I can't take any more of your constant remarks,
So I'm off to cool down in the park.
Don't you dare attempt to follow me,

"Please," I beg, *"just let me be."*
So off she went for an hour or two,
But then returned to use the loo.

The Dentist

Blast it all!
I'll have to give in.
It hurts so much,
It's hard to grin.
Let's bite the bullet,
Give up the fight.
On this occasion mother's right.
The only option is
To have a filling!
So, open wide,
And let's get drilling.

The Skiing Trip

Perfect skies, perfect snow,
Two wooden planks and off we go.
"How does this work?" I start to cry,
"There's nothing to it," came the loud reply.
"Just bend those knees and point those skies,
At your age, it should be a breeze."

"Oh my God!" I yell as I start to move,
I note my skies are in a grove.
They stay completely flat and rigid,
But my groove has a bend within it!
"How do I turn!?" I scream in rage.
"Why don't you start to act your age?"

It happened so quickly; I couldn't think,
The groove went left, my skis went clink.
The rock I'd hit was fairly small,
And my legs shot apart before the fall.
I'd been on snow for such a short while,
But somehow, I had lost my smile.

Felix

Felix, our cat, is rather dim,
I'm not sure why we purchased him?
He has no idea what is going on,
I'm pretty sure his mind has gone.
"Come here," I called one sunny day,
As Felix slowly walked my way.
However, what he hadn't seen,
Was next door's dog looking rather lean!
It was all over very quick,
Oh God! That cat was really thick!

Sleeping Beauty

As the title would suggest to me,
This little girl was a real beauty.
And trying to protect her dear,
The king and queen acted in fear.
They invited others to bless the child,
But left out the witch who wasn't mild!
On discovering this little fact,
The wicked witch was forced to act.
"I'll turn up and grant her a wish," she said,
"That little girl will soon be dead."
So, much to everyone's surprise,
The witch appeared with evil eyes.
She granted a wish to everyone's dismay,
That the girl would prick her finger one day!
And the result would be so very sad,
The little girl did not look glad!
"As soon as she pricks herself that day,
The child's breath will go away."
The congregation let out a sigh,
"Are you suggesting that my daughter will die?"
The cackling laugh gave the answer, alright,
But before they could grab her, she shot out of sight.

The three good witches, who had watched the affair,
Promised the king they would always be there.
"I'll make sure that curse does not come to pass,
Although she'll have to leave your kingdom, alas!"
The king and queen were really distraught,
And realised the lesson they had just been taught.
They should have invited the awful, wicked witch,
As resentment had created this terrible hitch.
So with heavy hearts, they agreed to the plan,
And off went their daughter with sandwiches of ham.
"We'll look after her," said Witch Number Three,
Then turned to the child: "That sandwich is for me."

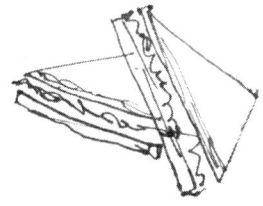

So into the night the carriage it sped,
And the little girl grumbled – she wanted her bed.
"No matter," said the witch, "we'll be there in a jiffy,
I'm sure you will find your new room very pretty."
So over the years, the little girl grew happy,
And the king and queen missed changing her nappy.
All grown up and into the forest she ran,
Singing as always of sandwiches of ham.
Then to her delight came a prince on an ass,
"Let's have a picnic – we can sit on the grass."
Oh, crumbs, thought the princess, he's after my lunch,
I'd better invite him over for brunch.
The witches fed him heartily, and as time came to pass,
The girl fell in love with the prince and his ass.

"Let's run away together," said the Prince with a plan,
"I can't!" exclaimed the girl. *"I'm in a real jam."*
Then explaining the problem, the princess she said,
"If I ever leave this place, I know I'll be dead."
"Don't worry," said the prince, *"we'll find a way,*
If I kill the witch, you'll never have to pay."
Although not sure it would work all that well,
The princess longed to be free from this hell.
So off went the prince on his newfound mission,
Taking some sandwiches with the princess's permission.
He reached the witch's castle the following day,
But his ass had stopped along the way.
On one such break, the ass talked to a bird,
And related the story which he thought was absurd.
What the silly ass really didn't know,
Was that this bird was no ordinary crow.
He belonged to the cruel and wicked witch,
To whom he related the news with a twitch.
So by the time they arrived at their destination,
The wicked witch had planned their cremation.
"Come in," she said with a wilful grin,
"You and your ass look rather thin.
Come sit and have a meal, both of you,
We're having roasted ham I hope it will do."

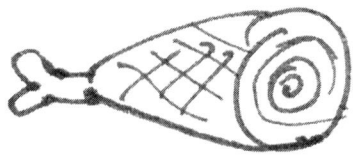

The joy that shone in the prince's eyes,
Masked any thought of the witch's lies.

So they sat and ate a lot of ham,
Then realised they were in a jam.
They both went very stiff and still,
But, before the witch could finish her kill,
The bird flew in, in a real state,
"At last, dear witch, she took the bait.
I saw her singing in the wood,
While nearby, all three witches stood.
We have the location – the search is done,
There's nowhere else for her to run.
I'll take back the potion and she'll follow me,
To the room where she will spin you'll see.
She'll prick her finger and die straight away,
Let's get it over with – today."
So back flew the crow with the potion pot,
And the poor princess fell for the lot.
It wasn't long before she was in very deep,
But instead of dying, she just fell asleep.
The rest of the castle soon followed that way.
And they all fell asleep on exactly that day.
Without any help, the castle fell into disrepair,
And got covered in branches without loving care!
During this time, the prince remained locked up,
But he managed to escape using a fork and a cup.
He made for the castle as quick as he could,
But realised the castle was covered in wood.
Then setting a fire to the branches around,
He made an entrance so Sleeping Beauty could be found.
He walked right up to her and kissed her on the lips,
Then slowly and carefully, she revealed her full hips.
It was clear that she'd eaten far too much meat,

And the prince tried to escape but was slow on his feet.
What he hadn't realised was that he had got old,
And the princess grabbed him in a very firm hold.
"At last!" she shouted, *"my prince is here,*
There's nothing left for me to fear."
Then, noticing the prince was so very old,
She decided to revert to being very cold.
"Why thank you, good man – I'll make sure you get a fee,
You see, I'm waiting for a young prince to rescue me."

The Prince for a moment realised his escape had come,
As he didn't want THIS princess and her enormous bum!

Famous Fred

Great fame came to my Uncle Fred,
Due to his enormous head.
It sat astride his lengthy shoulders,
Adopting the pose of several boulders.

Little children pointed at the sight,
While others ran away in fright.
But Fred enjoyed this type of fame,
Without his head, he would be plain.

The Maze

"*I know it's right,*" said Aunty Pat,
She didn't seem too sure of that.
For my part, I had no idea,
Both left and right filled me with fear.

I wanted food – I needed to eat,
"*Can't we rest our weary feet?*"
"*We can't stop now till we reach the middle,*"
"*But Aunty Pat, I need a piddle!*"

"*We're in a maze, you silly child,*
Your mother's made you far too wild.
You'll have to wait – we won't be long,
NO, don't turn left; that would be wrong."

So for an hour we walked around,
The middle it was never found.
And so with Aunty Pat in tow,
I said, "*It's time I have to go.*"
I couldn't stand it anymore,
And so I peed upon the floor!

Sunday Best

"Put on your Sunday best," she said,
I'd just got up and looked half dead!
What best thought I,
What can she mean?
She's not suggesting I look clean!
The weekend is for looking a mess,
For lying in late and wearing a vest.
She can think again!
I won't look clean.
Who does she think she is?
... The Queen!

The Big Bang

Mr Stephen Hawking's got it wrong, you know,
The BIG BANG didn't start the show.

Any fool could tell you how it started,
It all began when the blackness farted!!!

Sweets

Sweets glorious sweets,
Not just for birthdays or special treats.
Pink and blue and fizzy and sour,
I could eat them every single hour.
But Mum says that my teeth will rot,
She clearly knows I eat a lot.

I especially like them chewy and juicy,
And I eat them with my best friend, Lucy.
We spread our sweets upon the floor,
And share them out – no one gets more.
Then we start with red, then yellow, then green,
It's a spectacle like you've never seen.

At last, when all that's left are the wrappers,
We tiptoe out and scarper like the clappers.
There's no way we want Mum to see,
How utterly greedy we both can be.

Pinocchio

Geppetto carved his wood all day,
His job was hard with little pay.
Then one day while he carved away,
The wooden object began to flay.
This was followed by a little squeal,
And Geppetto realised this puppet could feel.
So he carved the wood into a toy,
And with a mouth and eyes, it became a boy.
Then much to Geppetto's utter delight,
The boy began to speak that night.
The problem was he was a naughty boy,
And this made poor Geppetto cry.
"Don't do that." shouted Geppetto in a rage,
"Or I'll have to put you in a cage."
On closer inspection, it soon became clear,
This little boy just couldn't hear.
So Geppetto carved him ears that day,
And Pinocchio was lost for words to say.
Staring up, he knew Geppetto would be his dad,
It was the very best present he had ever had.
But after some time, Pinocchio grew sad,
And it wasn't because he was unhappy with his dad
He decided he wanted to go to school,
But Geppetto said he was a fool.
"How am I supposed to pay for that?" he shouted

"Money is far too tight," as Pinocchio pouted.
But later after deep reflection,
Geppetto was filled with deep affection.
So off he went to sell his coat like a fool,
Gave Pinocchio a book and sent him off to school.
Unfortunately, Pinocchio was led astray,
He sold his book and visited the circus that day.
At the end of the act, Pinocchio found himself in trouble,
As Giovanni, the puppet master, had got into a muddle.
He grabbed for his puppets – taking Pinocchio away,
While planning to burn them as firewood that day.
After explaining the mix up, Giovanni gave him five coins,
"Take this to your father, Quick, boy, gird your loins."
So in haste, Pinocchio set to return to his dad,
But once again, matters turned out somewhat bad.
A cat and a fox tried to trick him indeed,
And he ended up paying for their afternoon feed.
Soon to be followed by a startling threat,
"Give me the rest of your coins or you'll live to regret."
So Pinocchio found himself hung from a tree
Only to be graced with a visit from a friendly fairy.
No sooner was he safe; he was again led astray,
And along with Carlos his chum, a price they would pay.
They were both turned into donkeys and sent out to work,
But Pinocchio got injured and felt such a jerk.
He was bought for his skin and thrown into the sea,
So he called out for help from his friend the fairy.
Once again, she saved him but all did not go well,
As unfortunately into a whale's mouth he fell.
Inside it was large and he wandered about,
Then much to his delight, he soon heard a shout.

His father Geppetto told how he had searched for his boy,
But a whale swallowed his boat as if it were a toy.
"We have to escape," said Pinocchio, trying not to cry,
"Don't worry," said Geppetto. *"I won't let you die."*
So they climbed out of the whale's mouth while he lay asleep,
But found that the water appeared very deep.
After swimming a while, they reached the shore,
And it wasn't too long before they reached their front door.
But the story is not yet at its end,
As the fairy who turned out to be Pinocchio's friend.
Called out while in trouble, so Pinocchio rushed to her aid,
And after sorting out the problem, the fairy then made.
Pinocchio a real boy for Geppetto his dad,
And promised that the future would never be bad.

The Oak Tree

"Hello," said Sam,
"I've come to play,
And take your acorns far away."

"Oh NO, you don't," the tree replied,
"These acorns stay,
They look just fine."

"I'm afraid to say you have no choice,
So put away that whinny voice.
My dad said it's okay to play,
And we need your nuts for Mum's display."

"Well, tell your mum to change her mind,
To steel my nuts would not be kind!"

Cheese

I love the type of cheese with holes,
It's like a garden full of moles.
You can carefully thread your finger through,
It's hard, yet squidgy – like quickset glue.
But the favourite part of all for me,
Is that it can be very smelly.

Night Creatures

That bump and bang as the lights went dim,
Always made me feel rather grim.
What makes the noise – I have no idea,
But I certainly think it's something to fear.
When I call my mum it seemed to end,
Maybe I'm going around the bend.
I can't think why it would come after me,
I'm harmless as a girl can be.
I pull the cover around my head,
My thoughts are full of total dread.
My breathing is so very slow,
I feel my pulse – it's very low.
Then just as I feel it's all alright,
I see the most horrendous sight.
My covers move at the end of the bed,
I close my eyes and wait in dread.
Then a soft and purring noise is heard,
And I squint in the light – it's very blurred.
Then Ginger comes and sits on me,
As happy as a cat can be.

Chinese Takeaway

I thought I ordered egg-fried rice,
But to my surprise, I checked it twice.
A little girl appeared to say,
Her name was Ingrid Price – Okay!
She informed me she had come to stay,
As China made her go away!

Rumpelstiltskin

My daughter ate all my pies today,
What drives her greed is hard to say!
It's like throwing income down the drain,
A problem which I can't sustain!
So to aid my anguish and let my rage be freed,
I began to sing of my daughter's greed.
Riding nearby, the king stopped with delight,
Assuming he'd heard my words alright.
"I heard you singing nice and bold,
Of your daughter's ability to spin her gold."
I therefore began to think it through,
Then realised, to agree was the thing to do.
Who was I to correct the king anyway?
I'd do his bidding on this perfect day.
"Tell me my king – what can I do for you?
Did you like my song or were you just passing through?"
The king gave out a little cough,
Then told my daughter they should be off.
"Go where?" she spluttered all at once,
I told the king she was such a dunce!
"No matter," said the king with glee,
"You should have heard the names my mum called me.
Your daughter must start to work at once,

It's irrelevant that she's such a dunce.
She can spin my straw into skeins of gold,
My kingdom will be a place to behold."
Oh God, I thought, *this could change my life,*
"But sir you will need to make her your wife."
I'll do it, thought the king in greed,
My debts are great – with this I'm freed.
So that very day, the marriage was blessed,
And I was thrilled to be a family guest.
Then three days passed and the king got bored,
He found it hard to sleep with the way she snored!
"My dear," said the king, *"Please follow me,*
There's something I want you to see."
So up the stairs she followed along,
Where she was greeted by an awful pong.
On closer inspection, it turned out to be,
A room full of straw that smelt of pee.
The door slammed shut – she was trapped inside,
There was no way out and nowhere to hide.
"Now spin my gold; I'm almost broke,
I'm not renowned as a patient bloke."
"What gold?" the girl said in complete surprise,
You could see the fear within her eyes.
"Your mother made it very clear,
Your talent can be fulfilled in here."
"Oh Crap!" she said as the penny fell,
My mother's responsible for this hell.
So she sat and cried and cried and cried,
At the fact her mother had lied and lied.
Then looking up, she saw a little man,
"Get out!" she screamed, *"as fast as you can."*

"I'm here to help," said the strange little thing,
"I'll spin your gold if I can have your ring?"
"A deal," said the girl with a happy heart,
"I'll pass you the straw; let's make a start."
Within a short time, all the gold was spun,
And the king was impressed by what she'd done.
So for the next few days, the spinning went on,
Until all the girls possessions had gone.
"I can't do anymore," said the little man,
This put her in a real jam.
"What can I do to change your mind?"
She had to escape this awful bind.
"You must make me a promise,
Or I will leave tonight.
Your first child will be mine,
That's my payment, all right."
"Fine," said the girl. *"Just get it done,*
We'll never have kids the king's no fun."
So the little man continued to spin and spin,
And the king continued to grin and grin.
Eventually, the king had all that he needed,
And he resumed his marriage as the girl had pleaded.
Then one year later, to both their glee,
Appeared a baby boy for all to see.
But sadly, the girl had forgotten the past,
And the little man appeared for the baby at last.
"Oh no," said the girl, *"this cannot be,*
Surely you'd prefer a fee?"
"A promise must be kept," said the little man,
"Now give me the kid as fast as you can."
After lots of pleading a deal was eventually struck,

And the little man said, *"You will need enormous luck.*
You must guess my name – let's seal this bet,
Or the debt that you made must be fully met.
I will give you three days, then the kid becomes mine,
Please don't continue to sob, beg and whine."
"Okay," said the girl, *"I'll discover your name,*
But the fate of my child should not be a game.
Is it Jack, George, Lewis or Phil?
Is it Jerome, Ken, Henry or Bill?"
And so on and on went the list of names,
And each time the little man disputed her claims.
Day One soon was over and the name wasn't found,
"Oh no," said the girl, *"to this promise, I'm bound.*
Is it Carlo?" said the girl with a desperate plea,
"Oh no," said the man, skipping with glee.
"What the hell can I do?" said the girl to a mate,
"Maybe the answer is to find him a date."
"No," said the pal, *"he would realise the trick,*
He may be small, but I don't think he's thick.
Maybe your best plan is to follow him tonight,
It's bound to reveal the answer to your plight."
"Great," said the girl, *"what a splendid thought!*
I'll send my best servant – he'll never get caught."
So later that evening, to the girl's delight,
The little man sang out his name in the night.
When eventually he arrived on the final day,
The girl sat smiling in a confident way.
"Is it Fred, John, Alex, Benjamin or Finn?
Or perhaps it's RUMPELSTILTSKIN!"
With sheer astonishment, the little man stood still,

"How did you find out?" he screamed with a terrible shrill.
"That's not part of the deal," said the girl with glee,
"Now leave this kingdom or I'll make you flee."

Baby Goo

"Ooh and aah, my little bundle,
Here comes the train; let's open the tunnel."

"What train? What tunnel? Are you insane?
That stuff should go straight down the drain."
No better still, let's have some fun,
Not all us kids were born so dumb.

Giggles, bubbles, that jumper's new,
Not looking so good; now it's covered in goo!

Chocolate Pie

It's time for tea,
That pie's for me.
It's a perfect fit,
For my tummy!

Let's eat it hot,
I'll scoff the lot.
My mum is wrong,
My teeth won't rot.

The Washing Up

"You wash – I'll dry,"
No time for my reply.
"It's fast – You'll see,"
No answer still from me.
"Can you please collect the plates?"
That's one of my pet hates!
"First one to the kitchen is the winner,"
Then we'll do the same again for dinner.

My Dog

I promise if I can have a pet,
I'll do all the chores that you have set.
I'll walk her each and every day,
And only feed her when you say.

She'll never sleep upon my bed,
And she'll stay in the kitchen to be fed.
She can have a blanket on the floor,
It won't cost much, of that I'm sure.

We could get her cheap from a rescue vet,
Oh please, I really want a pet.
But there's one thing I don't want to do,
Perhaps you could clean up her poo.

ICT

They say this is the future,
But I'm afraid, I disagree.
The use of my computer,
Frustrates the life from me.

Unlike the many levels,
On which your brain relies.
My electronic brainchild,
Has nothing to decide.

It merely follows sequences,
And, as anyone can see,
Those sequences are not the same,
As the ones inside of me!

Naughty Girls and Naughty Boys

Naughty girls and naughty boys,
Spend lots of time destroying toys.
So imagine one fine and sunny day,
When Henry, a good child, came to play.
He arrived in time to see a sight,
Which gave him such a dreadful fright?
The building blocks had been set on fire,
And smoked in the grate like a funeral pyre.
Nearby, there stood the charred remains,
Of many dolls who had lost their brains!
It's time to escape – I'm not staying to play,
Let's run for the door and skip away.
But sadly, Alex had different plans,
And smiled with glee and clapped his hands.
"That toy you have inside your pocket,
Would be great to use as a flaming rocket."
"Oh, no you don't," Henry said straight away,
"I only bought it the other day.
It can stay where it is – I'm not giving it you,
You're raving mad – God knows what you'll do!"
"Don't worry," said Alex all very coy,
"We'll choose another toy to destroy."

Frog – Not a Prince

"Let's kiss a frog – it's bound to work,"
"Don't be so dim; you're such a jerk!"
"Look, fairy tales suggest it's true,
They're old and wise – not daft like you."
"Go on then. Be my guest, you fool,
That frog will cover you in drool."

A kiss she planted on his check,
And, as foretold within a week.
My reservations came to pass,
A hairy wart appeared – alas!

Safety Zone

My mother's constantly on at me,
About my need to act safely.

I'm not sure why she's so concerned,
My SAFETY FIRST, I have already learnt.

I look both ways before I cross the road,
And I never carry an enormous load.

She thinks I must be accident prone,
And tries to surround me with a safety zone.

The Palm House Quiz

I wrote this poem for my daughter's birthday-party quiz which took place in the palm house at Kew Gardens. All the plants highlighted in bold can be found there. A poem and a quiz – maybe give it a try when you visit?

My mother, with her caring ways,
Said, *"Wear your vest this rainy day."*
Oh drat, thought I, *how very naff,*
Let's hope my friends don't start to laugh.
My cotton vest stuck to my back,
She obviously didn't think of that!
"It's time for tea" I heard her cry,
My hopes were dashed – I'll tell you why.
She'd started spicing all my food,
From now on, fish was never nude.
On sausages or mutton mash,
On crispy pork or corned beef hash.
The **pepper** used was very hot,
I know my stomach soon would rot.

"Sit at the table and wash your hands,"
Another of her many demands!
The table was as black as black could be,
And hard to sit at and eat your tea.
*"It's made of **ebony**,"* she said,
"It's harder than your wooden head!"
The only saving grace would be,
The pudding she had made for me.
The **sugar** cane was still in lumps,
But easily spotted by the bumps.
A little bit was nice and sweet,
But eat too much and your dead meat!
Now, while we ate this sugary treat,
My mother thought it rather neat,
To burn some smelly incense stick,
It made the air so very thick.
*"It's **ylang ylang**,"* she called out in glee,
It made me want to run and pee!
It had the heady sort of aroma,
Which could easily put you in a coma?
Next came the final dollop of food,
And although I did not want to be rude,
It looked just like a slimy bog,
I wondered if I'd find a frog.
"It's fresh and fruity and good for you."
It shone of yellow gloppy glue,
*"You'll love the **mango**; it's a treat."*
The **star fruit** floated like rotten feet!
I spooned it in with an air of dread,
Then noticed the arrival of my Uncle Fred.
I saw him walk towards the kitchen,

Then all of a sudden, he was missing.
Then came a loud and frightening din,
As Fred slipped on a **banana** skin.
"I'll make a stretcher," Mother said,
"I'll just nip out into the shed."
So there with **giant bamboo** sticks,
Which weighed as much as household bricks.
She produced a contraption so very wide,
That Fred's demise was no surprise.
He was crushed like a feather with all that weight,
My mother put it down to fate.
"I'll call the funeral parlour," she said,
"My darling poor old uncle Fred.
The wreath we choose will need to be red,
*No wait; I'll use **frangipani** instead*
Its aroma is heady and very hot,
Your Aunty Lucy can pay for the lot.
I think a burial at sea,
Would be as fine as fine can be?
*Let's float some **passion flowers** about,*
Fred's favourite food was deep-sea trout!
I know the spot where the seats could be,
*It's right beneath the **cannonball tree**.*
Then afterwards, I'll prepare a supper,
I'll need to bring my pressure cooker.
I'll make us all a delicious feast,
*With **paw paw** and **coconut** from the east.*
The beach will be a perfect spot,
Dear old Fred sat there a lot.
*Underneath the battered **rubber tree**,*
He'd gaze into the deep blue sea.

He'd languish inside his panama hat,
Joined by his very faithful cat.
*He'd sit and sip his cup of **coffee**,*
And suck upon his favourite toffee.
Unfortunately, as you will see,
The only drawback there will be,
Is that the beach is home to many,
Flowers that are green and smelly.